SAM STEELE

Tony.K.
FROM
Yeri & Shoyro
Christmas 2005

AMAZING STORIES

SAM STEELE

The Wild West Adventures of Canada's Most Famous Mountie

HISTORY/BIOGRAPHY

by Holly Quan

PUBLISHED BY ALTITUDE PUBLISHING CANADA LTD.
1500 Railway Avenue, Canmore, Alberta T1W 1P6
www.altitudepublishing.com
1-800-957-6888

Publisher   Stephen Hutchings
Associate Publisher   Kara Turner
Editor   Lori Burwash
Digitial Photo Colouring   Scott Manktelow

We acknowledge the financial support of the Government
of Canada through the Book Publishing Industry Development
Program (BPIDP) for our publishing activities.

Altitude GreenTree Program
Altitude Publishing will plant twice as many trees as were used
in the manufacturing of this product.

National Library of Canada Cataloguing in Publication Data
Quan, Holly
  Sam Steele : the wild west adventures of Canada's most famous mountie /
Holly Quan.

(Amazing stories)
Includes bibliographical references.
ISBN 1-55153-997-7

1. Steele, Samuel Benfield Sir, 1849-1919. 2. North West Mounted Police
(Canada)--Biography. 3. Police--Canada, Western--Biography. 4.
Northwest, Canadian--History--1870-1905. I. Title. II. Series: Amazing
stories (Canmore, Alta.)
FC3216.3.S77Q36 2003   971.2'02'092   C2003-910167-3
F1060.9.S82Q36 2003

An application for the trademark for Amazing Stories™
has been made and the registered trademark is pending.

Printed and bound in Canada by Friesens
4 6 8 9 7 5 3

The front cover shows Sam Steele aged 22.
All photographs are reproduced courtesy of Glenbow Archives.

To the memory of Frank Brown, who embodied the wit, character, and presence of Sam Steele. Ride on.

Contents

Dawson City

Yukon River

KLONDIKE

Mt. Steele

YUKON

NORTHW
TERRITO

Lake
Bennett

Chilkoot Pass

White Pass

Skagway, Alaska

N

W   E

S

ROCKY MOUNTAINS

ALBE

BRITISH
COLUMBIA

Fort Saskatch

Edmo

CANADIAN PACIFIC RAILWAY

SELKIRK
MOUNTAINS

Golden

PACIFIC

OCEAN

Vancouver

Victoria

Kootenay Post
(Fort Steele)

Crowsnest
Pass

0   100   200   300   400
KILOMETRES

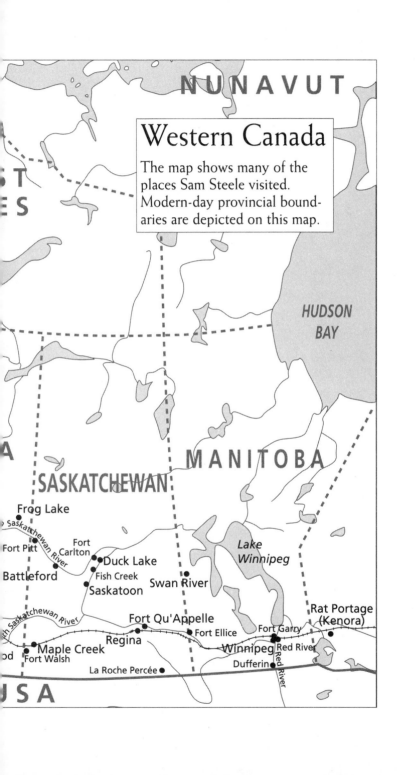

NUNAVUT

Western Canada

The map shows many of the places Sam Steele visited. Modern-day provincial boundaries are depicted on this map.

HUDSON
BAY

MANITOBA

SASKATCHEWAN

Frog Lake

Saskatchewan River

Fort Pitt   Fort Carlton

Duck Lake

Battleford   Fish Creek

Saskatoon   Swan River

North Saskatchewan River

Lake
Winnipeg

Rat Portage
(Kenora)

Fort Qu'Appelle

Fort Ellice   Fort Garry

Regina   Winnipeg   Red River

Maple Creek

Fort Walsh   La Roche Percée •   Dufferin   Red River

USA

Prologue

Steele's Scouts travelled all day through rough country, finally coming to the North Saskatchewan River valley. It was approaching midnight — men and horses needed to rest, so Sam Steele halted his troops and told them to wait. He asked two riders to help him find a suitable camp, and the three men rode down the slope into the dark valley.

Cautiously, Sam and his men probed through the bush. They came upon a promising clearing, an open area of tall grass that appeared to offer protection from surprise attack. Sam softly murmured, "This is just the thing."

Suddenly to Sam's right, a rifle blazed and a bullet buzzed past his head. Then a second shot! The bullet burned through Sam's sleeve. The Scouts drew their arms but could see nothing in the dark, while their startled horses reared and bucked. A Cree sharpshooter, concealed in darkness, was shooting at them. Just as Sam took aim with his pistol, one of his men rode forward and raised his own rifle, cracking off a shot. The warrior fell dead in the tall grass.

The woods were instantly alive with gunfire. Mounted Cree fighters, screaming battle cries, seemed to materialize straight from the night itself. Sam's two companions cursed and shouted, riding between Sam and the Cree warriors and firing into the tangle of shadows and movement. Afraid he'd hit his own men in the noise and confusion, Sam couldn't return fire. Rifle fire, brilliant as lightning, blinded both Scouts and Cree. Time seemed to freeze, but it was all over after only 60 seconds. Vanishing as quickly as a summer storm, the Cree disappeared into the dark.

For Sam Steele and Steele's Scouts, it was just a taste of things to come.

Chapter 1
A Dose of Adventure

am Steele was a lifelong adventurer. Driven by a restless energy, he looked for excitement and challenge around every corner.

As a boy, Sam practically lived outdoors. He spent his spare hours in the woods around his father's farm, exploring, tracking, hunting. As a teen, he lived in Orillia, Ontario, where he learned to ride and shoot under the patient, watchful eye of an older brother. But town life lacked the action Sam craved, so he joined the militia and went to Fort Garry during the Red River Rebellion. That trip gave Sam his first dose of real adventure — and set the stage for the rest of his amazing life.

A Bold Young Man

When he retired from the British Navy in the 1840s, Captain Elmes Steele, his wife, Elizabeth, and their six children thought they would live the high life in the sunny south of France. It didn't turn out that way. The French unrest came to a boil, and Captain Steele decided there were safer places. So he moved his family to Simcoe County, in what was then known as Upper Canada (now Ontario). The British government gave him a large land grant, and he started a new life as a gentleman farmer.

In 1846, only a few years after the family moved to Canada, Elizabeth Steele died. Captain Steele soon remarried and with his new wife, Anne, began a second family. Their first child, Samuel Benfield Steele, was born on the family farm on January 5, 1851. Sam's education started early and he remained an avid reader throughout his life. Though there was no school in the district, the Steele home was filled with books, and Elmes and Anne tutored their children at home. Sam excelled as a student, but after his lessons and farm chores were done for the day, his real love was roaming the vast wild woodlands around the farm. He learned to swim and fish, and he loved tracking animals and building shelters of branches and moss. It was a young boy's paradise, and Sam grew tall, strong, athletic, and observant.

When Sam was just 9 years old, his mother died, and Captain Steele moved his family to the nearby town of Orillia. But after two years, he returned to the farmstead, leaving his younger children, including 11-year-old Sam, in Orillia under the care of John Steele, the eldest son from his first marriage.

For the next three years, John was a major influence on Sam. Perhaps sensing the spark of adventure in young Sam, John tried to give the boy the tools and skills necessary for a life of excitement and challenge. Thanks to John's teaching and discipline, Sam, already a natural athlete, became an excellent rider and marksman.

Captain Elmes Steele died in 1865, an uneasy time in Upper Canada. Fierce Irish Americans called Fenians were trying to promote Irish independence from Britain by attacking British territories in North America. Residents in small, isolated towns such as Orillia felt vulnerable to the Fenian cross-border raids and looked for volunteers to act as militia defenders. With his bold character and large stature, 14-year-old Sam had no difficulty convincing the local recruiters that he was 16 and old enough to enlist.

Sam travelled to Toronto to take officer training. Again he excelled, scoring top marks in drills and discipline. He returned to Orillia a trained militia officer, but he didn't see any battle action. By 1867, the Fenian threat was over and the new Dominion of Canada was born. Sam hung up his soldier's uniform and found a job as a store clerk in the nearby village of Clarksburg. That might have been the end of his military career, but events in Manitoba, a small settlement in the distant North-West Territories, were about to open a door in young Sam's life.

In 1870, distrust and discontent among the Métis erupted into an armed uprising led by Louis Riel, a passionate believer in Métis rights. To put down the Red River Rebellion and restore order to the Red River settlement, the Dominion government called up the militia. Among the first volunteers was a bored and restless store clerk named Sam Steele.

Simcoe Sam

Sam was assigned to a company called the First Ontario Rifles. Although he had the training and qualifications to be an officer, he wanted to remain in the ranks and get a taste for the true life of a soldier. By June 1870, the militia was ready to move west to fight Riel and the Métis. More than 2200 troops, 19-year-old Sam among them, set off on their western adventure.

The journey was an exercise in endurance. The troops marched across southern Ontario to Sault Ste. Marie, where they boarded ships bound across Lake Superior to what is now Thunder Bay. That was the easy part. From the lakehead, 965 kilometres of rock, rivers, muskeg, and heavy forest lay between the troops and their destination, Fort Garry on the Red River (now Winnipeg). There was no railway yet, and the road was nothing more than a trail blazed through the bogs and bush. In fact, for the most part, the "road" was a water route of interconnected lakes and streams with numerous difficult portages through mud, swamps, and dense forest.

It was Sam's kind of trip. Despite the hardships, he thoroughly enjoyed the experience. He loved the thrill of rocketing through white-water rapids and welcomed the hard work. Over the numberless portages, he carried his own pack plus additional supplies — the combined load was equal to the weight of a man — proving himself strong and willing. More than anything, Sam took great delight in the companionship of his fellow soldiers, who nicknamed him Simcoe Sam.

Because the route was so difficult, it took the

troops more than two months to get to Fort Garry. When they finally did arrive — on August 29 — the rebellion was over. Riel had escaped to the US. The Métis people remained distrustful of the Dominion government, but with their leader in exile, their anger simmered down, at least temporarily. For the men of the militia, who had just completed a long, arduous journey, there was nothing to do but turn around and go home to Ontario before winter set in.

A Taste of the West

Not wanting to return to the quiet life of small-town Ontario, Sam remained at Fort Garry, where a small garrison was to stay behind to keep the peace. He soon learned that although Fort Garry seemed exotic and exciting, it was only the tip of the western iceberg.

As Sam met and talked to soldiers, traders, settlers, and travellers, he developed an image of the vast, wild North West. He heard tales of native warriors and huge buffalo herds, whisky traders and horse thieves, towering mountains and sweeping plains. To the ears of ambitious young Sam Steele, the Wild West sounded like a fantastic place. He longed for a way to venture farther west, but it was beyond his reach — Sam's duties were with the militia. From the beginning, Sam was a disciplined soldier who wouldn't dream of disobeying an order, much less deserting the militia to pursue his appetite for adventure. So he stayed put in Fort Garry.

Early in 1871, Sam was promoted to corporal and transferred to another company. In this new position, he supervised a collection of tough characters, most of them much older. The men disliked their eager young commander and did everything they could to test his mettle. Sam had no end of trouble keeping this rough bunch in line, but he was a big man, and tough as nails — their taunting, insubordination, and sneering disdain didn't faze him. Then, one night, the toughs discovered that Sam Steele was just as tough as they were.

Sam was off duty, hanging out in the barracks with a number of his men. A big-boned private named Kerr was cleaning the stove and clowning around with the cook. Kerr took a playful swipe at the cook and got some black stove polish on the cook's nose. "You couldn't do that to me," shot one of the other soldiers. "Sure I could," replied Kerr — and suddenly a fight was on. Grabbing a knife, the soldier stabbed Kerr in the thigh. He made a second lunge at Kerr, who grabbed heavy cast-iron stove tongs and hit the soldier on the head, knocking him cold. The man thudded to the floor like falling timber.

The noise brought the soldier's belligerent friends

storming into the room to find Kerr bleeding from his thigh and their buddy unconscious on the floor. They were intent on beating Kerr to a pulp, but Sam snatched up a rifle and stood in their way. Swearing at him, the soldiers started to advance. Although the gun wasn't loaded, it was still an efficient weapon in Sam's hands. He swung the butt end of his rifle, driving the men back through the doorway and down the stairs. For the first time, Sam understood how to use his size, combined with quick action, to sway a touchy situation in his favour.

Throughout the year, Sam continued to train and discipline his troops, who now had considerably more respect for him. Meanwhile, local political events took an ugly turn during the first election campaign in the brand-new province of Manitoba. Bitter feelings between settlers and Métis continued to trouble the Red River settlement. Things came to a head on election day, November 29, 1871, when there were riots and fighting as each side tried to intimidate the other. Tension mounted and the garrison's troops were assembled and ordered to load their muskets with live ammunition.

The situation could have escalated into a bloodbath, but the steady nerves and cool thinking of the commanding officers kept the peace, and the election proceeded. Sam, ever the careful observer, learned another important lesson: to resolve a tense situation, reserve and judgment are preferable to force and violence.

Once the new provincial government was established, the remaining militia were relieved of their duties and made their way east. With a taste of lively frontier life, Sam chafed. He simply couldn't return to a dull civilian job. Instead, he joined the army.

British troops had long been Canada's keepers of internal law and order and defenders against outside enemies, but the young Canadian government wanted its own made-in-Canada armed forces. Upon his return to Ontario, Sam was the 23rd man to enlist in the new Canadian army. He was sent to Fort Henry, near Kingston — no doubt believing he was embarking on a lifelong career as a soldier.

Chapter 2
Red Coats
in the West

S am Steele was well on his way to making a career in the Canadian army, but when the North-West Mounted Police was established in 1873, he saw his chance to go west again. He spent most of the next decade chasing criminals, defying native leaders, upholding the law — and having the time of his life.

A Police Force for the West
At Fort Henry, Sam loved everything about military life — the discipline, the uniform, the challenge. He espe-

cially enjoyed the companionship of like-minded men from all sorts of backgrounds, their stories of adventure, their dreams of glory. Sam impressed his superiors and earned a reputation for honesty and trustworthiness. But army life wasn't enough. Sam longed for real adventure and action. He wanted to go west again.

In 1873, Sam saw his chance when he heard rumours that Prime Minister Sir John A. Macdonald was about to establish a mounted police force for the West. But first Sam had to get out of the army. He went to see Colonel George French, the commanding officer at Fort Henry, who was only too happy to oblige Sam's request. French had just been appointed commissioner of the newly named North-West Mounted Police (NWMP), and by releasing Sam from the army, he would still have the impressive young soldier under his command. French promptly gave Sam honourable discharge, and Sam immediately volunteered as a recruit for the NWMP.

The North-West Mounted Police was officially established with the passing of an Act of Parliament on May 23, 1873. Over that summer, there was plenty of work to do. French had to find suitable recruits, outfit them (with, among other things, bright red jackets similar to those worn by the militia), and round up all sorts of supplies, from tents and cooking pots to rifles and ammunition. Then men and equipment would have to make the arduous journey to their new headquarters at Lower Fort Garry (north of present-day Winnipeg).

Because of his militia background and experience in training and drills, Sam was given the rank of sergeant-major and put in charge of some new police recruits. On October 6, Sam and his men started their journey to Lower Fort Garry. Once again, Sam boarded a boat and steamed to Port Arthur at the lakehead, then continued overland. The road and river journey was just as troublesome as his 1870 passage. Despite the tough conditions, the police recruits made good time, arriving at Lower Fort Garry on October 22, just days ahead of a killing cold spell.

Sergeant-Major Sam

It was time for Sam to start training his recruits, forging police officers from the unlikely assortment of individuals who had enlisted. He didn't waste any time. Many men quickly grew to dislike him for his hard-driving and apparently callous ways. Sam forced his troops to practise drills for hours on end in all kinds of weather. Throughout the winter of 1873–74, he worked them relentlessly in temperatures as cold as -37° Celsius.

Sam never asked his men to perform a task he wouldn't undertake himself, and he knew he couldn't spare his men. The recruits had to be prepared for difficult days, riding long patrols on the open range. They had to be ready for anything from bad weather to hostile Native peoples, whisky traders, horse thieves, and more. Sam intended to make sure they would be top-notch riders and excellent marksmen — physically fit enough to withstand whatever they encountered.

Before Sam could begin teaching his men to ride, the recruits had to train the half-wild horses the government had supplied. An exceptional rider himself, Sam had little patience for the greenhorns under his command and showed no favourites when it came to the difficult task of getting a horse to accept a bit and saddle. One day, after a recruit was bucked from his horse and the horse stepped on him, Sam yelled to the other recruits to "look after that poor horse, and carry that awkward lout off the square!" The "lout" was none other than one of Sam's younger brothers.

Even though he had their best interests at heart, Sam was an incredible taskmaster. Many recruits simply couldn't keep up. Some deserted (recruits agreed to sign on for three years, and desertion was a crime punishable by prison). Others were discharged because they were not fit for service. Although the Act that established the police called for a force of "not less than 300 healthy men," the initial body of men at Lower Fort

Garry dwindled to just 120, an insufficient number given that Sam himself thought the task of policing the prairies called for at least 1000 men.

Clearly, the mounted police needed more recruits and better horses. Colonel French went to Ottawa and returned in June 1874 with more than 200 fresh recruits and 244 well-bred horses. These men took a different route west from Ontario, travelling by rail through the United States to Dakota, then marching to the settlement of Dufferin, just north of the border. Meanwhile, the police from Lower Fort Garry made ready to march south to rendezvous with the new recruits. Sam organized the march, a journey of 130 kilometres, and on June 7, they left Lower Fort Garry, dressed in their red jackets, flags flying.

Almost as soon as Sam and his men arrived at Dufferin, the new recruits got a taste of what hardships their life on the plains would hold. On the second night, the horses from Ontario were penned in a crude corral made of circled wagons and Red River carts. A huge thunderstorm rolled in and lightning spooked the herd. The tough western ponies were accustomed to such violent weather and stayed put, but the new horses were terrorized. They broke through the barrier of wagons and stampeded south over the plains. Losing the new horses was bad enough, but to make matters worse, they headed toward hostile Sioux territory across the border. At dawn, the men dispersed in search of their scattered horses. Sam himself covered 180 kilometres on horseback that day. It took two days to round up the horses. Incredibly, the men found all but one.

At last, on July 8, 343 troops pulled out of Dufferin to begin the Great March West. According to French's plans, the police would build forts throughout the West. They were also supposed to establish farms so they could be self-sufficient, raising enough food for themselves and their horses. Consequently, as the troop started out from Dufferin, they took with them a herd of cattle, spare horses, and an extensive train of Red River carts and wagons loaded with everything from cooking pots and farm implements to guns, ammunition, and artillery. The train stretched about 4 kilometres. With upright military bearing on his horse, Sam Steele led his A Troop. He was 23 years old and living his dream of adventure in the West.

Quicksand and Cold Water

Although the Canadian West was not as lawless as the American frontier, it was still full of danger and unrest. Sam was one of the few new recruits who had a clear idea of the dangers that awaited them.

The troops were heading straight into native territory. The Assiniboine roamed what is now southern
Saskatchewan, with Plains Cree to the north and Woods
Cree in the bushlands farther north. The Blood, Peigan,
and Stoney lived to the west, and the Blackfoot claimed
ancestral lands from Montana to Edmonton and as far
west as the Rocky Mountains. The Blackfoot Nation was
as fearsome and dangerous as the Sioux or Cheyenne in
the US.

As the great buffalo herds diminished, the traditional native way of life was changing drastically across
the prairies, leaving many Native people feeling threatened and powerless. In desperation, they turned to
whisky — a concoction that included anything from
kerosene to ink. In theory, alcohol was banned throughout the West, but in fact it was easy to come by.
American hunters freely traded their noxious home
brew for furs and buffalo hides. Drunkenness and alco-
holism were devastating native societies, frequently
leading to fights, shootings, and murders, and creating a
volatile situation for the new mounted police.

Nature was a formidable enemy, too. As the troops
rode west, they encountered scorching heat, clouds of
biting insects, drenching rain, mud, swamps, treacherous river crossings, and bad drinking water. Grasshoppers ate everything in sight, leaving no forage for the

horses and cattle. Still, the troops battled their way across the plains. Animals became weaker, and many men became sick with dysentery and heat exhaustion.

At the end of July, the group came to a crossing of the Souris River, at a place called La Roche Percée. Located about one-third of the distance between Dufferin and the Rockies, La Roche Percée (meaning "Split Rock") was named for an odd man-sized opening in a large rock on the river's bank. Here, Colonel French brought the march to a halt, partly to rest his weary entourage, partly to decide what to do about the orders he'd just received by mounted messenger. French was to send a party of men to Fort Edmonton, a Hudson's Bay Company (HBC) trading post and small settlement on the banks of the North Saskatchewan River, more than 1400 kilometres away.

French decided to split his men into two groups. Inspector Jarvis would take a division from A Troop, including Sam Steele, and head north to Fort Edmonton. The sick men and horses would go with them. Colonel French and the Great March continued west on July 29, leaving a tiny detachment of men from A Troop behind at La Roche Percée.

Sam was disappointed but, always a disciplined soldier, he followed orders. As the last of the wagons and carts disappeared over the western horizon, Sam turned his attention and energies to getting his men, supplies, and horses to their new destination.

On August 3, Jarvis and his entourage set out northward. The group included 12 healthy men from A Troop plus 12 sick men, a herd of weak horses, a large herd of oxen and cattle, and numerous heavily loaded supply wagons and carts. Their first objective was Fort Ellice, an HBC post about 160 kilometres away. But the going was tough for the already beleaguered group. Grasshoppers razed the grass, and rain turned the wagon track to deep mud. Quicksand was another hazard many men had never experienced. Sam, among the strongest in the troop, was continually called on to help wrestle horses, oxen, and cattle out of boggy deathtraps.

One day Sam's own horse jumped unwittingly into a bog full of quicksand and instantly sank up to its neck. As the horse went down, Sam leaped from the saddle, landing face down in the shifting sand. While his horse continued to struggle and sink, Sam "swam" toward his terrified mount, grabbed the reins, and gently coaxed the horse. The animal pushed its way through the thick sand toward Sam, who kept pulling calmly on the reins. When Sam reached firmer footing, he backed away from the pit, encouraging the horse until it safely hauled itself onto solid ground. He then remounted and continued the journey.

It took 11 days to cover the distance to Fort Ellice, where the sick men and undernourished animals remained. The rest of the troop carried on to Fort Edmonton but ran into even more challenging conditions. Still having little grass to eat, the horses became so weak they collapsed in their tracks. The men had to lift the fallen horses and encourage them to walk a little farther before they fell once again. "I lifted horses forty times a day," Sam later wrote in his autobiography.

The men didn't fare much better. They had insufficient rations, too, surviving on primarily hard biscuits and beans, supplemented by fish and game shot along their route. Besides lifting horses, they also had to keep the exhausted, footsore cattle moving, wearily chasing strays that wandered from the herd. The men continually had to build temporary log roads over the worst of the mud holes, and their normally bright red jackets were tattered and filthy, their high leather boots — meant for riding — were no match for walking across the endless prairie.

Despite their hardships, or maybe because of them, the men forged strong bonds as they shared stories around their nightly campfires. The Métis wagon drivers entertained the troops with fiddle music and step dancing — one had even brought along a door, which he laid flat on the ground so he could dance on it.

The troop finally reached another HBC post, Fort Carlton, on September 11. By this time, the Métis drivers were tired of the rough conditions and staged a strike. They were set to go home, which would have been a disaster for the police — the troops had enough on their hands with the weak horses; there wasn't a man to spare for driving wagons. Luckily things blew over when the officers, including Sam, talked the Métis into continuing with the northbound journey. And the strike had a small benefit: men and animals got a short rest at Fort Carlton while the issue was resolved.

After a week, the troops hit the trail once more. The layover did little to revive the ailing horses though, and continuous rain turned the trail into endless mud. Again and again, the undernourished horses fell and couldn't get up. At night, the men covered the wet, shivering animals with their own blankets and rubbed their legs to keep their circulation going. As the days wore on, the men not only had to lift horses, but were often obliged to literally carry them by putting a pole under an animal and helping it walk along, half carrying, half dragging it. Sam was usually on one end of the pole. Yet somehow the troop's good humour prevailed. One of Sam's companions quipped, "I thought I'd have an easy ride to the Rockies with a good horse to carry me. Instead I'm having a tough walk to Edmonton, with me carrying the horse!"

The police eventually reached Victoria, a tiny trading post and settlement east of Fort Edmonton. With fresh horses, Jarvis took a party of men and rode ahead to Edmonton, leaving Sam in command of the sorry herd. The final push from Victoria to Fort Edmonton was even tougher, with horses constantly collapsing. At each mud hole, the wagons had to be unloaded. The men then pulled the empty wagons through the bog, reloaded, and carried on a few hundred metres to the next mire. Some sloughs had already iced over, but the ice was too thin to support the horses, so the men had to drag animals out of frigid water using ropes and poles.

By October 31, Sam and his men were less than 20 kilometres east of Edmonton. Though men and horses were weary beyond belief, Sam's orders were to make it to Edmonton that day. Relentlessly he pushed on until five o'clock in the morning, when they were just 8 kilometres from their goal. However, the group simply could not continue, and they stopped for some rest, rolling out their blankets under the wagons.

Sam was preparing for sleep when someone shouted that a horse was in trouble in a nearby creek. Grabbing a rope, he waded into the ice-cold stream and deftly passed the rope around the struggling horse, tossing the other end to men on the bank. But before Sam could get out of the water, the horse slipped, dragging Sam and several men down. In the dark, with only moments before both men and horse succumbed to the freezing current, the quick-thinking group conducted an heroic rescue. First one man made it out of the water, then he hauled the next man out, and so on, until troops and horse were all free of the ice and water.

While his men slept, Sam remained awake, cutting poles. When Inspector Jarvis rode into camp later that morning, Sam was cheerfully building a bridge over the creek that had almost claimed several lives. Jarvis roused the troops and they continued the journey to Edmonton. Gratefully, the tired men arrived in the settlement where they were to spend the winter. Sam and his men had travelled 2000 gruelling kilometres since leaving Dufferin.

The men settled into a life of maintaining law and order along the North Saskatchewan River, mostly raiding whisky traders. Meanwhile, the main body of the North-West Mounted Police that had continued west with Colonel French was busy building its regional headquarters on the Oldman River. The post was called Fort Macleod for the commanding officer, Assistant Commissioner James Macleod. Among the first visitors to the post was the Blackfoot chief Crowfoot, who told the mounted police they and their laws were welcome.

In Fort Edmonton, Inspector Jarvis was also busy with construction ideas. He began drawing plans for a permanent NWMP post at Fort Saskatchewan, about 30 kilometres northeast of Edmonton, believing the proposed Canadian Pacific Railway would be routed through that location. (He was dead wrong — the rail route went through Calgary, more than 300 kilometres to the south.) Come spring, he put Sam in charge of the fort-building project. By early summer of 1875, the job was done and the police moved into their new post.

At that time, Edmonton was served by paddle-wheelers that came up from Lake Winnipeg, bringing supplies and mail to remote communities. When the season's first steamer arrived, it brought news that Sam was promoted to the rank of regimental sergeant-major, along with orders for him to report to the NWMP headquarters at Swan River in Manitoba. Sam retraced almost the entire distance back to where he had started a year earlier, with serious misgivings. Was he destined to spend his police career training recruits in Manitoba? Was this the end of his Western adventure?

Luckily, Sam's anxieties were short-lived. In June 1876, after training recruits for a year, he was ordered to return to the West and spent the next two years at a number of NWMP posts. He rode long patrols through the plains and foothills, chasing rustlers, whisky traders, and common criminals. He also witnessed the signing of important treaties between the Dominion government and two First Nations: Treaty Six with the Cree Nation and Treaty Seven with the Blackfoot.

In May 1878, the NWMP headquarters moved to Fort Walsh, near today's Alberta–Saskatchewan border. While stationed at Fort Walsh, Sam continued training new recruits and led numerous patrols. It was difficult and often tedious work, but Sam's performance earned him a promotion to the rank of subinspector — an officer at last.

"The Man Behind You Is Freezing to Death!"
In January 1879, Sam turned 28 and, at that time, was considered middle aged. Sam was anything but middle-aged, though — he was tall, broad-shouldered, and barrel-chested, a powerful man in top physical condition. His long stride and resounding voice commanded attention and respect. With his piercing dark eyes and the flourish of his mustache, he cut a dashing figure.

However, the rigorous conditions Sam endured in the course of his ordinary duties frequently tested his mental and physical toughness. Now posted in Calgary, he was put in charge of conducting a census of Métis living between Calgary and Fort Macleod. He set out with two constables, Holtorf and Mills, a Métis guide and interpreter named Foley, and what should have been plenty of food and hay. Sam estimated the task would require no more than a week, including travel, because Fort Macleod was only 240 kilometres southeast of Calgary. But the snow was deep and the temperature severe, and the men made little progress on the first day. Then a blizzard howled in on the second day. Deciding to wait out the storm, the four men dug a shelter in the snow. They were there for two full days.

Finally the storm was over. Sam and his men attempted to continue their journey, but the snow was deep and drifted. Their progress was very slow, made worse because the snow had covered familiar landmarks. Despite the Métis guide's knowledge of the area, they lost their bearings. After nine days, they ran out of food, but Sam estimated they were still at least 60 kilometres from their destination. They had to keep going.

The men continued without food for three more days. The horses, also without food and exhausted from pushing through deep snow, grew increasingly weak. Then another blizzard struck. Sam knew that if they stopped, they would surely die of cold and hunger, so he rode on through the swirling snow, leading his men more by intuition than by knowledge. Suddenly his horse refused to walk on, yet Sam could see nothing ahead. He dismounted and took only a few steps forward. That's when he realized the horse had halted just short of a steep slope. With a little reconnaissance, Sam discovered they were above the Oldman River. The stubborn horse had saved his life, and Sam now knew where they were. Fort Macleod was only about 30 kilometres away.

At last the horses could go no farther, and Sam decided to make camp for the night. The next day, they abandoned two of the horses. Holtorf mounted behind Sam, Mills doubled on Foley's horse, and they rode on. The storm was intense and Sam was concentrating on finding the route — he wasn't paying attention to the young constable mounted behind him. Suddenly Foley rode up alongside and called through the screaming wind, "The man behind you is freezing to death!"

Sure enough, Holtorf was only half conscious and slowly losing his battle with the intense cold. Sam pulled the nearly comatose man to the ground, slapped his face, and shook him violently while shouting in his face, "You are too young to die yet!" Holtorf revived enough to get back on Sam's horse, but no sooner had the party set out than Sam noticed that Mills, mounted behind Foley, was about to meet the same fate. Shouting to Foley, "The man behind *you* is freezing to death!" Sam stopped and smacked Mills back into consciousness.

And so it continued, with first one constable then the other losing consciousness. Finally Holtorf was too weak and disoriented to get back on the horse. At that fateful moment, Sam smelled smoke on the wind and knew they were close to a ranch house. Rousing Holtorf enough to make the stricken man walk, Sam supported his constable as they struggled through the snow to the house. The rancher's wife helped Sam and Foley get the other two men wrapped in warm blankets and gave them hot soup. Without Sam's determination, both constables would have died of exposure.

The next day, Sam and Foley rode the remaining 6 kilometres to Fort Macleod, where they arranged for an ambulance to pick up the constables. Sam also sent men to bring in the horses he'd abandoned the day before. But the original purpose for Sam's trip still remained undone, so Sam and Foley rode out once again to complete the Métis census, which they accomplished in just a few days. The mission, however, took them twice as long as expected.

A Voice from the Forest
Big Bear, a Cree leader, was restless. So were some of his followers — Wandering Spirit in particular. One of Big Bear's leading warriors, Wandering Spirit was a ruthless

man who would attack and rob anyone when he got the chance, including other Native people. In the winter of 1879, he had surprised some Cree hunters and stolen their food and horses. A Métis man discovered the Cree hunters and their families on the open plains, destitute and helpless, and took them to Fort Walsh. Sam was then commanded to mount a patrol to capture Wandering Spirit.

The police searched near where Wandering Spirit had attacked the hunters. After three days, they found his camp on the Red Deer River, but night was falling, so Sam and his patrol camped warily nearby. At first light, Sam split his men into small groups, and they surrounded Wandering Spirit's camp while remaining hidden in the bush. When his men were in place, Sam gave the signal and they swooped down on the sleeping camp, only to find that Wandering Spirit was not there. The police arrested everyone in the camp, and Sam directed some of his men to escort the prisoners to Fort Walsh. Meanwhile, Sam took 14 men and continued to look for Wandering Spirit.

Searching along the South Saskatchewan River, Sam and his men discovered a second camp, which they again silently surrounded in the dim evening light. To the surprise of Wandering Spirit, who was in one of the teepees, a voice boomed from the dark woods, commanding him to come out with his hands up. It was the deep, resonant voice of Sam Steele. Wandering Spirit obeyed and was placed under arrest.

Back at Fort Walsh, Wandering Spirit was sentenced to several months in jail for his attack on the Cree hunters. When released, he went north to join Big Bear. It was not the last Sam Steele would see of Wandering Spirit.

Rocky Mountain Fever

Sam Steele must have seemed invincible. Tough trails, quicksand, and dangerous creek crossings had not deterred him. Cold could not conquer him. Wily native warriors could not outwit him. But Rocky Mountain fever nearly stopped Sam in the prime of his life.

In the summer of 1879, Sam was posted at Fort Walsh, where his star continued to rise — he was promoted to inspector. Among his duties was the sad task of distributing flour and other supplies to starving Native peoples on reserves in the area, in addition to riding patrols to seek out the ever-present and watchful whisky traders. One day when he was on patrol, his horse stepped in a gopher hole. Sam was thrown and shaken up but stayed on duty, unlike the horse, which was put to pasture to recover.

Perhaps Sam was weakened from his fall, or perhaps he had finally met his match. He came down with the first of his two battles with Rocky Mountain fever, which is similar to typhoid. The illness is caused by bacteria borne by ticks, and symptoms include sudden fever, headache, and muscle pain, followed by a rash and escalating fever. In the days before antibiotics, Rocky Mountain fever was often fatal. Many men at Fort Walsh fell victim to the fever, and several died. Sam was bedridden for a few days, but seemed to recover, and resumed his duties before he should have. Hearing that a friend was ill with fever and near death, Sam rode to the man's homestead to see whether he could help. But his friend died shortly after Sam left. As soon as he got back to Fort Walsh, Sam collapsed and was placed in the post's infirmary. This time, Rocky Mountain fever had the upper hand.

Sam's temperature was dangerously high, and he was delirious. He was on death's door, or so the attending doctor thought. Leaning over the bed, the well-meaning physician kindly asked Sam if there were any requests or last wishes for his family in Ontario. Sam replied that he had no last requests because he had no intention of dying. The doctor shook his head and departed.

Constable Holtorf — the young man whose life

Sam had saved in January — volunteered to take care of Sam during his dying days. Finally, one night it looked as though Sam's time had come. Convinced that Inspector Steele was about to breathe his last, Holtorf lay on the floor beside Sam's bed to be near his mentor when death came knocking. But he didn't know Sam Steele. Sam awoke in the middle of the night and asked Holtorf what he was up to. When the young constable told him, he laughed out loud — albeit weakly. "Go back to bed and let me get some rest," Sam gruffly instructed. He made a full recovery.

Chapter 3
Railways and Rebellions

B y the early 1880s, Sam Steele was riding high, in charge of his life and his destiny. He was bold and decisive, a man of action. He sometimes garnered criticism for making up rules as he went along, but he was always willing to take that chance. Sam Steele was the law in a lawless land.

Steel Rails Across the Prairies
By early 1882, Sam, now posted at Fort Qu'Appelle (in what is now southern Saskatchewan), had earned a long

vacation and headed east to see his family in Ontario. On a stopover in Winnipeg, he received orders to set up an NWMP recruiting office in his hotel room. The Dominion government had decided to increase the NWMP force from 300 to 500, to help keep the peace as the Canadian Pacific Railway (CPR) was built across the plains. Eventually the prairie section of the railway would stretch more than 1400 kilometres, from the bogs and muskegs of the Canadian Shield to the distant Rocky Mountains.

Sam was obliged to stay in Winnipeg until spring, reducing his long-awaited vacation to only a couple of weeks. When he returned to Fort Qu'Appelle, he was ordered to follow the "end of track" as the railway slowly stretched across the prairies, keeping law and order in the railway construction camps along the line. The camps were occupied not just by rail workers, but also by whisky sellers, gamblers, prostitutes, and assorted other riffraff. There were other perils for the railway, too. Native peoples and Métis throughout the West saw the CPR as a threat to their traditional ways. As well, those who had settled on various reserves were outraged because the government was not living up to promises made in the treaty agreements. Many First Nations threatened to block the railway or tear up track to get the government's attention.

However, Sam's most pressing problem was controlling the availability of alcohol. The North-West Territories were under prohibition, but whisky could legally be made in Manitoba and across the border in the US, then smuggled into the construction camps. The many bootleggers were resourceful when it came to hiding and transporting their goods. They filled hollowed eggs with liquor, disguised kegs in sacks of grain and barrels of salt, even ripped the pages out of Bibles and substituted mickeys of alcohol. It took all of Sam's resourcefulness and energy to stay a step ahead of the crafty whisky traders.

During the summer of 1882, the CPR employed 4000 men on the plains, but Sam had just 30 police under his command. Despite the limited manpower and resources at his disposal, Sam managed to keep tight control over the flow of whisky in the camps. His efforts came to the attention of the CPR's general manager, William C. Van Horne. At the end of the 1882 construction season, Van Horne wrote a glowing letter of commendation to Sam's boss, NWMP Commissioner Irvine: "The North Western Mounted Police, whose zeal in preventing traffic in liquor and preserving order along the line under construction, have contributed so much to the successful prosecution of the work. Without the assistance of the officer [Sam Steele] and men of this splendid force ... it would have been impossible to have accomplished as much as we did."

As the railway continued its westward progress, the NWMP's headquarters was moved to Regina. Sam spent the winter of 1882–83 in Regina, overseeing construction of the new post. He was also now a magistrate, presiding over Regina's courtroom.

Determined to complete the line across the prairies and into the Rocky Mountains by fall 1883, the CPR's managers increased the work crew to 5000 men that spring. Trouble erupted almost as soon as construction started in April. Workers at Maple Creek went on strike and the CPR fired them. An angry mob of more than 100 threatened to wreck the camp and tear up track. Tempers heated as a striker roughed up a construction foreman. Sam arrived at the scene and arrested the striker. He sent the man to jail in Regina, telling the remaining strikers they would face similar punishment if they took any further violent action. Grumbling, the men went back to work, but the event was a hint of the unrest bubbling just under the surface at the rail construction camps.

Through the summer months, Sam moved up and down the line, keeping watch over the goings-on as the end of track approached Calgary. In the middle of all this, Prime Minister Macdonald personally summoned

Sam to resolve a problem at Rat Portage (Kenora) that had nothing to do with the railway. Both Manitoba and Ontario claimed the region, and both provincial governments had appointed local magistrates. The fight escalated when each tried to have the other arrested and residents took sides. Even the Dominion government couldn't resolve the issue.

Macdonald referred the dispute to the Privy Council in London, believing it to be an impartial authority, and ordered Sam to Rat Portage to keep the situation under control until a decision was rendered. But Sam's reputation for no-nonsense law and order was enough to quell the trouble. When the feuding residents learned that the famous Sam Steele was on his way, their tempers cooled. Sam had travelled only as far as Winnipeg when he received word that his presence in Rat Portage wasn't necessary. To be safe, he was ordered to remain in Winnipeg for a short time in case trouble broke out — but it never did.

A Murderer Goes to Trial

In November, Sam was posted to Calgary for the winter of 1883–84. Calgary was a roaring, prosperous frontier town with all the attendant social problems — drinking, gambling, and prostitution. Sam Steele has the distinction of being the first person in Calgary's history to close down a brothel. He charged two women, Nellie Swift and Nina Dow, with keeping "a house of ill-fame" and gave them two choices: six months in prison or take the next train out of town. They left.

But the biggest problem Sam encountered that winter was solving a murder. Jim Adams ran a mercantile shop and sometimes extended credit to his customers. Among them was Jesse Williams, one of the few black people living in Alberta at that time. One afternoon, Adams and Williams were seen having a heated argument about money. Soon after, Adams was found dead in his shop, his throat cut — Williams was the alleged culprit. Having a murder to solve was one thing, but Sam also had to deal with smouldering racial prejudice. The situation called on Sam's skills as a police officer and magistrate, and on his cool head and sound judgment.

The mounted police arrested Jesse Williams and held him in the Calgary barracks of the NWMP post. An angry mob gathered outside, bent on grabbing and lynching the prisoner. This was not the first time Sam had to face a furious horde, and as usual he did not hesitate. Dressed in his red jacket, his fierce eyes blazing, Sam stood before the jostling crowd and yelled, "There has never been a lynching in Canada, nor will there be as long as our force has duties to perform. So go away like sensible men, and remember that any attempt at lynching will be bad for those who try it!"

Initially, the case against Williams was circumstantial. Investigating police found overshoe tracks in the snow around Adams's shop, but there was no proof they were Williams's footprints until Sam discovered conclusive evidence of his guilt. When Williams was brought to the barracks, Sam noticed that the bottom of the prisoner's right trouser leg was frozen stiff and left a mark in the snow. Sam found the same mark amid the footprints behind Adams's shop. Williams was convicted of murder and hanged at Fort Calgary on March 29, 1884.

Entering the Lion's Den

Ever since the Red River Rebellion of 1870, when Sam first went west, the Métis' old misgivings and grudges against the government had festered. Louis Riel had been living in exile in Montana, but in 1884 he secretly recrossed the border. Once back in Canada, Riel began building support for the Métis cause, sowing the seeds of a second rebellion.

Sam learned that a Métis agent of Riel's was on the Blackfoot reserve east of Calgary. This man, known as Bear's Head, was half Cree. Although the Cree were traditional enemies of the Blackfoot, Bear's Head was living among the Blackfoot, enticing them to join Riel's planned revolt. Chief Crowfoot appeared to be listening.

Sam sent two mounted police officers to Blackfoot Crossing east of Calgary to arrest Bear's Head. They caught him and were returning by train when he escaped by jumping from the train. Never one to back down or let a criminal get away, Sam himself rode out to find the fugitive. At his side were two constables and a Métis interpreter.

Sam and his men arrived in the middle of the Blackfoot's sun dance, a ceremony that had attracted hundreds of Blackfoot people from throughout southern Alberta. Sam boldly entered Chief Crowfoot's teepee, where he found Bear's Head among the leaders. Through the very nervous interpreter, Sam first told Crowfoot that he had come to arrest Bear's Head, then in English he told the escapee to come along peacefully. The Blackfoot sat staring at Sam. Bear's Head made no move to comply. The atmosphere was thick with anger and tension.

Suddenly Crowfoot lunged. Sam barked to the Blackfoot chief to hold his ground. With incredible audacity, Sam then strode over to Bear's Head and grabbed the Métis agitator by the collar, keeping his other hand ready over his revolver, then he dragged

Bear's Head outside, where the two constables were waiting. As they tied Bear's Head to their wagon, the police were surrounded by hundreds of angry Blackfoot warriors, shouting threats and brandishing weapons. Sam stood on the wagon and, with the not-too-willing help of the interpreter, addressed the warriors. He told them that when the mounted police had a job to do, they would not stand for interference by any man, white or native. He then called for Crowfoot to come out of his teepee.

Amazingly, the savvy Blackfoot leader emerged from his lodge. Sam berated Crowfoot for breaking his promises to respect the law. Then in front of Crowfoot and the gathered warriors, Sam accused Bear's Head of lying and trying to make trouble. He invited the chief to the agitator's trial in Calgary to see for himself that Bear's Head was bent on dragging the Blackfoot into war in support of Riel. The police and their prisoner then left the scene with no further trouble.

Bear's Head stood trial in Calgary but was discharged for lack of evidence. Still, the seeds of unrest had been planted. Were the Blackfoot about to join Riel?

The Riot Act

In 1884, despite Sam's growing concern about native

and Métis unrest near Calgary and the potential for an uprising, Sir John A. Macdonald personally requested Sam to continue policing the CPR's construction, now well into the Rocky Mountains.

The mounted police had control over a narrow strip of land 16 kilometres wide on either side of the track. Inside this police zone, gangsters, gamblers, shady ladies, and drinking establishments were forbidden. However, whisky traders, gambling houses, and brothels sprang up all along the advancing line, safe just outside the zone. To complicate matters, once the railway extended into British Columbia, liquor was legal. The provincial government, seeking tax dollars, was happily issuing licences to anyone who wanted to open a bar.

Sam had just 25 men under his command. Undaunted, he started another energetic and thorough campaign to rid the railway line of undesirables. One of his first tasks was to protect the CPR's payroll from the threat of armed robbery. Sam set up routine patrols along the rail line, paying special attention to the many potential ambush points in mountain country. He also asked the Dominion government to expand the police zone to a width of 60 kilometres (30 kilometres on either side of the track), which the government promptly proclaimed.

Sam's men did most of the patrolling and arresting, while Sam himself was judge and jury. In October 1884 alone, he prosecuted 67 cases for crimes ranging from vagrancy to illegal gambling. It was clear to the riffraff in the construction camps that Sam Steele ruled with an iron fist.

Ever so slowly, the end of track inched toward the crews building eastward from the Pacific coast. At the close of construction in 1884, the end of track was near a settlement called Beaver, deep in the looming Selkirk Mountains. Beaver was a town of tents and shanties housing 700 construction workers, plus a collection of legitimate and illicit businesses, from barbers to brothels. The NWMP post, Sam's office for the winter, was on the settlement's outskirts. Sam's crew had been reduced to only eight.

Big trouble was brewing. The railway was in financial difficulty again. The CPR couldn't pay contractors, who in turn couldn't pay their workers. By Christmas, most men in the camp hadn't been paid for weeks, and there was talk of a general strike. The starving men began stealing from the CPR and from one another, yet somehow Beaver's bars, brothels, and gambling parlours did a booming trade, often on credit. Liquor flowed freely — it wasn't unusual for 30 drunks to be in the police cells after a busy night.

Sam, fearing an outbreak of violence if the workers decided to strike, sent a telegram to Prime Minister Macdonald informing him of the volatile situation. However the government was in no position to come up with more cash to pay the CPR. Tensions in Beaver mounted as winter dragged on and the rail workers went without pay.

In the spring of 1885, Rocky Mountain fever struck the settlement, including the NWMP detachment. Sam himself fell victim and was once again ravaged by the disease's debilitating symptoms. Meanwhile unrest in Beaver came to a head on April 1. While rumours circulated that Sam was bedridden and near death, rail workers walked off the job. Then Sam received a telegram ordering him to take all his men from Beaver and proceed immediately to help put down the Métis rebellion that had finally erupted on the plains. Riel had made his move.

It was one of the few times in his career that Sam Steele disobeyed an order. He was too sick to travel — besides, the situation at Beaver was close to exploding. Sam replied by telegram to his superior officers that he intended to stay right where he was.

Leaning heavily on a constable's arm, Sam struggled into a chair and met with the strike leaders. He warned them to control their men and advised them to negotiate with the CPR and the construction contractor, James Ross. This the workers did, and Ross made some concessions. A few men decided to return to work, but not everyone was satisfied with Ross's deal. About 300 armed strikers set out from Beaver, determined to prevent the strikebreakers from going back to their jobs.

At a nearby half-built bridge, strikers confronted workers. The strikers destroyed some equipment, then at gunpoint ordered the workers to lay down their tools. The terrified workers swiftly boarded a waiting work train with contractor Ross in the locomotive. Ross commanded the engineer to move ahead through the shouting mob of strikers. As the train pulled forward, the strikers fired their revolvers, but Ross pushed ahead and the train made it safely through, headed back to Beaver.

With Sam desperately ill, it fell to Sergeant William Fury and three police officers to face the crowd and prevent further violence. The red-coated officers positioned themselves across the tracks where the workers' train had just passed, bravely facing the enraged strikers. Fury told the strikers to desist, and the grumbling throng turned back to Beaver. Fury then returned to the police post to tell Sam what was happening. Sam again struggled to a chair to formally hear Fury's report, then dismissed the sergeant.

Fury left but returned after just a few minutes to

tell Sam there was more trouble. Sam had sent a constable to fetch some medicine from the CPR supplies. On his way back to the NWMP post, the constable encountered the strikers, led by a man named Behan. The constable tried to arrest Behan, but the crowd attacked the police officer, who barely escaped a severe beating. Sam replied, "We must take the man at any cost. It will never do to let him or the remainder of the gang think they can play with us." He told Fury to take whatever men he needed and go into Beaver to arrest Behan.

Fury and three men found Behan and his followers in a saloon. The police tried again to arrest Behan and again were unsuccessful. They retreated to the NWMP police cabin, where they got no sympathy from Sam, who told them, "Take your revolvers and shoot anyone who interferes with the arrest."

Fury and his men, now armed and with instructions to use their firearms as necessary, returned to the centre of Beaver. At the sound of gunshots from town, Sam's companion at the post, Dr. George Johnston, commented, "There is one gone to hell, Steele." Sam staggered to the window to see two constables hauling Behan to the post, with Fury and the other constable performing rear guard, keeping the screaming strikers at bay.

At the sight of his men in trouble, Sam threw on his

red tunic and cried to Johnston to bring a copy of the Riot Act. He then grabbed a rifle, yanked open the cabin door, and, despite his weakened condition and high fever, strode out into the fray. The strikers, on the far side of the footbridge separating the NWMP post from Beaver, began their charge. Sam reached the bridge and brought his rifle into position. "Halt or I shall mow you down!" he yelled.

The crowd was awed at the giant man who appeared to have risen from the dead, and hung back. One worker muttered, "Look at the bastard. His own death bed makes no difference to him." Johnston arrived with the Riot Act in hand. Sam stepped onto the bridge and shouted, "Listen to this and keep your hands off your guns or I will shoot the first man of you who makes a hostile movement!" He then told Johnston to read the Riot Act, which among other things made it illegal for groups of more than 12 individuals to assemble. Then Sam spoke to the crowd again, saying, "I warn you that if I find more than 12 of you standing together or any large crowd assembled I will open fire! Now disperse at once and behave yourselves." After a few tense moments, the standoff dissolved and the strikers retreated.

That night, Sam sent the prisoner Behan to another post to avoid further violence should the crowd try to set him free. The next day, he fined the mob's ring-leaders $100 each, then took a train to where Behan was being held and gave him the same punishment. All this while suffering from Rocky Mountain fever. Sam again made a full recovery.

As the Riel Rebellion exploded on the plains far to the east of Beaver, the CPR suddenly found itself able to provide a vital service — transporting more than 3000 troops from Ontario to quell the rebellion. Funds from the resulting government contract pulled the railway from the edge of financial disaster. The workers were paid. The strike was over. But the Riel Rebellion was on.

Rebellion!
While Sam was handling the strike at Beaver, events on the prairies developed rapidly. Riel had declared himself leader of a provisional government, and the entire West was on the brink of war. Ranchers, farmers, traders, even residents of towns and cities were afraid not only of Riel and his Métis followers but of the First Nations that threatened to join the revolt. Suddenly, law and order in the North-West Territories seemed tenuous at best, and rumours about raids, gunfights, even murders were rampant. People were on edge and believed what-ever wild stories they heard.

On March 26, 1885 — just days before the events in Beaver — Riel and a band of 200 followers defeated police and local volunteers at Duck Lake (in what is now Saskatchewan). Although Crowfoot so far had resisted leading the Blackfoot Nation to join Riel, many Cree and Assiniboine took up the fight, looting and burning several Hudson's Bay Company trading posts. The day after Sam put down the riot at Beaver, Wandering Spirit led a band of Cree warriors against a tiny settlement of settlers at Frog Lake, northeast of Edmonton. The Cree murdered nine people including two priests. They took two women as hostages and carried on to the NWMP outpost at Fort Pitt, where 20 mounted police and a number of settlers were barricaded against Big Bear and his followers.

Among those inside Fort Pitt were the McLeans, old friends of the Steele family. W. J. McLean was a trader with the HBC, and the McLean family had lived at several trading posts throughout the West. The police force at Fort Pitt was commanded by Inspector Francis Dickens, son of Charles Dickens. By mid-April the tiny garrison could not hold off Big Bear's attack. The civilians, led by W. J. McLean, surrendered to the Cree, while Dickens and his men evacuated the fort and fled down the river to Battleford.

On April 11, Sam was finally able to obey the orders

he'd received on April 1. He headed to Calgary as the events at Frog Lake and Fort Pitt unfolded. When he arrived, Calgary was in uproar. Rumours that Crowfoot would lead the Blackfoot Nation against the city had citizens fearing a war. The train station was jammed with women and children evacuating to safer places both east and west.

Prime Minister Macdonald was sending troops from the east to fight Riel, but many able-bodied men already in the west were ready to take up arms. Various troops, police, militia, and volunteer soldiers came forward in defence against the Cree and Métis. The man appointed to command this motley army was Thomas Strange, a retired general from the British Army. Strange lost no time in requesting that Sam be temporarily discharged from his regular duties with the NWMP to be second-in-command. Sam suddenly found himself a major in the Alberta Field Force, Strange's instant militia. He was to command the cavalry unit, which Strange named Steele's Scouts.

As it turned out, fears that the Blackfoot would join the uprising were unfounded. Crowfoot remained neutral, and Calgary was safe from attack. Meanwhile, though, Big Bear and Wandering Spirit, leading a band of approximately 600 Cree warriors, were in control of the territory northeast of Edmonton. Isolated farmers and traders in that region were in grave danger. Even residents of the area's towns and villages weren't much safer, with no police or other protection. The makeshift army under Strange's command was to ride against Big Bear while General Middleton led an army of troops from eastern Canada against Riel.

Sam got busy recruiting seasoned men to ride with him, mostly cowboys and mounted police, including Sergeant Fury and the entire NWMP detachment from Beaver. Also under Sam's wing were a contingent of militiamen from Quebec and another 20 mounted police from Fort Macleod, who brought with them their cannon. In all, Sam had about 60 men under his command.

Over the next few days, Sam had to train his cavalry, find adequate supplies and horses, even find uniforms. The North-West Mounted Police had their traditional red jackets, but Strange wanted the troops to wear something less conspicuous. He came up with a rather ridiculous suggestion, asking Sam whether the mounted police could wear their tunics (which were lined in brown) inside out. "My men are not turncoats," Sam laughed. However, he took the hint and found suitable camouflage clothing for the Scouts, outfitting them in brown canvas jackets and broad-brimmed hats similar to the Stetsons the cowboys wore. Unfailingly proud of his NWMP uniform — and not about to give it up, even in the interests of safety — Sam wore his red tunic throughout the campaign.

On April 20, Strange was ready to march north, with Steele's Scouts in the lead. Sam later recounted, "The start in the morning was like a circus. The horses, with few exceptions, had never been ridden and bucked whenever mounted until two or three days had gentled them." General Strange compared the plunging, bucking parade to something out of Buffalo Bill's Wild West Show.

On that same day, Middleton fought Riel at Fish Creek in Saskatchewan — and lost. Over the next week, while Middleton's troops reorganized for a renewed assault, Strange continued leading his men toward the rendezvous with Big Bear. Their northward march was a difficult one. All the rivers and creeks were in spring flood, and crossings were treacherous. In addition, Sam noticed signal fires and mirror flashes and knew unfriendly Native peoples were shadowing them.

The militia reached Edmonton on May 1. The next leg of their march led east toward Frog Lake. Sam had been through this rough, swampy territory 11 years before, when he and the men of A Troop literally carried their horses to Fort Edmonton. He knew only too well how difficult their trail would be through the bogs and bush. By May 24, the troops reached Frog Lake, where they recovered and buried the bodies of the murdered settlers and priests. Next they carried on to Fort Pitt. When they arrived two days later, they found the mutilated corpse of NWMP Constable Cowan, who had been shot by the Cree.

Now Sam was faced with a dilemma: Which way had Big Bear gone? South, to join forces with Poundmaker, another Cree leader who had taken up with Riel? Or north, into the vast and trackless bush?

Sam spotted faint wagon tracks and footprints leading north from Fort Pitt, but that wasn't enough evidence for a decision on which direction to take. General Strange was ready to head south, and several of his advisers agreed with him, but Sam was unconvinced. Searching in the bush just north of the fort, Sam noticed a piece of paper on the ground. Unfolding it, he recognized it as a letter Mrs. McLean had shown him a number of years before, when he'd visited the McLean family at one of their HBC postings. Sam surmised that as the hostages surrendered to Big Bear, she had grabbed a few prized possessions, then deliberately dropped the letter as a clue for the rescuers she hoped would be on Big Bear's trail.

The letter was all the proof Sam needed that Big Bear was headed north. Strange agreed and gave Sam orders to pursue the Cree and their hostages. The Scouts rode hard all day in an effort to catch up with the Cree, who had a considerable head start. That night, Sam and two Scouts were involved in a brief gun battle with Cree warriors. It was a close call, and the Scouts spent a wary night watching for more trouble. One thing was certain — Big Bear and his followers were not far away.

The next day, Steele's Scouts continued on the trail and found Big Bear's recently vacated camp. Sam knew they were tailing a large band of Cree and estimated that the Scouts were outnumbered by perhaps 10 to 1. As Sam and his men investigated the camp, an advance group of Scouts came galloping back with a number of Cree in hot pursuit. Sam instantly ordered his dismounted men to form a firing line, but as the native warriors approached, they slowed and turned away. Sam realized the Cree had planned a second ambush, foiled by the advance Scouts. Evidently Big Bear was a clever leader who was using all his tricks.

May 28: The Battle of Frenchman's Butte
Knowing how outnumbered his men were, Sam waited for Strange, the other troops, and the artillery to catch up. The entire ragtag army then advanced slowly through the quiet of the late spring afternoon, Steele's Scouts in the lead. They found their quarry at a ridge called Frenchman's Butte.

Despite the desperate situation, Sam retained a great respect for his adversaries. He later wrote, "Their excellent horsemanship and wild appearance making a remarkable picture as they were silhouetted against the sky and disappeared over the ridge top." As the Cree vanished from sight, Steele's Scouts pressed forward through dense bush, but dark was falling, so the troops circled their wagons and prepared for another wary night. As May 28 dawned, Sam and his Scouts advanced stealthily on foot. Approaching the base of Frenchman's Butte, Sam saw that the Cree had a tremendous tactical advantage because the ground at the ridge's base was swampy while the hillside was covered in heavy brush.

As the Scouts left the shelter of the dense bush and tried to cross the boggy ground, Cree marksmen began firing down on them from carefully concealed rifle trenches. Luckily, the native shooters were armed with old or inadequate rifles, so the Scouts were able to reach the cover of bush and begin working their way up the hill. Meanwhile, Strange's troops were pounding the ridge top with cannon fire.

Strange ordered Sam to take some Scouts back to their waiting horses and ride around behind the ridge and the enemy camp while Strange and the remaining troops kept the Cree occupied on the hill. Sam tried this

Railways and Rebellions

tactic, but the Cree had guards surrounding their camp and the Scouts could find no way through. The Scouts retreated, and Sam recommended that they try to get around the Cree rifle pits from the other direction. At that moment, one of Sam's men, who had climbed a tall tree, reported that the Cree riflemen were leaving the hilltop trenches and running to their camp on the far side of Frenchman's Butte.

However, despite putting the enemy to flight, Strange had to retreat. His troops were running out of ammunition, and Strange was nervous about camping a second night with the potential for a surprise attack. In frustration, Strange withdrew, and the entire militia force returned to Fort Pitt.

June 3: The Battle of Loon Lake

At Fort Pitt, General Strange learned that General Middleton's forces had defeated Riel at Batoche on May 12, more than two weeks before the battle at French-man's Butte. Regardless of Riel's defeat, Big Bear and Wandering Spirit were still at war and held 25 hostages. With Riel's fires extinguished, Strange expected Middleton to bring his infantry to Fort Pitt to help defeat Big Bear. Strange waited for two days, but Middleton and his army failed to appear. Exasperated, Strange sent

Sam back to Frenchman's Butte to see if Big Bear was still in the vicinity.

The Cree camp was deserted, but Sam did find furs, supplies, and booty the Cree warriors had looted from Frog Lake and Fort Pitt. The plunder had been left behind as the Cree hurriedly fled their camp after the battle, obviously fearing that Strange's army was right behind. Sam realized that the cannon fire had routed the Cree, who panicked and ran in disarray. If Strange had had enough ammunition to follow, the Cree uprising might well have ended that day.

Sam sent word to Strange that he intended to follow Big Bear's trail once more. The Scouts were concerned for the hostages' safety, especially the women. Sam was particularly worried about the McLeans, though he knew the Cree had great respect for W. J. McLean, whom they called Straight Tongue.

Sam was eager to proceed but waited for approval from Strange, so made camp. That night — June 1 — the Scouts found five captives wandering in the woods. They had been freed by some of Big Bear's more reluctant followers, Woods Cree who had left the warring party. The freed captives told Sam that Big Bear, his warriors, and the remaining hostages were moving northeast. A messenger arrived with word from Strange that Steele's Scouts should continue chasing Big Bear but that Strange himself had orders from Middleton to stay at Fort Pitt.

When he got these instructions, Sam wasted no time pursuing Big Bear. It was two o'clock in the morning, but Sam roused his sleeping men by shouting, "Get up men, get up! Take eight days' half rations and all the ammunition you can and follow me!" Then he mounted his horse and galloped off. All day the Scouts proceeded through rough country, along a barely discernible trail that the fleeing Cree had made even more difficult by setting fires and dragging trees across the track.

On June 2, General Middleton and 200 men finally arrived at Fort Pitt, where Strange and his troops were impatiently waiting. By then, Steele's Scouts were far ahead in the heavy bush. Strange requested that Middleton send troops immediately to reinforce the Scouts, but Middleton — a British Army veteran who did things by the book — denied the request, saying, "Not a man! Not a man! Who is this Major Steele? It should not have been done!" Eventually, however, Middleton saw the wisdom of Sam's relentless pursuit of Big Bear and agreed to follow with his soldiers.

Far to the north, Sam and the Scouts continued to trail Big Bear. Sam found several more notes from McLean saying the hostages were all right and the Cree war party had turned to head northwest. The Scouts knew they were close behind the retreating band. Relentlessly, they stayed on the trail from noon until just before dawn on June 3. As the men rested, an advance party found the Cree camp and sent word back to Sam, who led his men through the bush in the early morning light.

Crawling quietly to the top of a ridge, Sam looked down on Loon Lake and the Cree camp on its shore. He estimated there were 200 warriors, fewer than before but still outnumbering the Scouts by more than 3 to 1. Sam summoned Canon MacKay, who spoke Cree, and was in the middle of telling MacKay to call for Big Bear to surrender when Cree scouts discovered the hiding troops and opened fire. Instantly Sam leaped to his feet, drew his revolver, and began running downhill toward the camp, yelling to his men to follow. Steele's Scouts, whooping and firing, stormed down the hill, flushing the Cree sentries.

As the Scouts got to the bottom, they split into two groups. One carried on into the camp, the other circled to the right. The Cree warriors fled their teepees and scattered into the bush. Some tried to outflank the Scouts, but Sam sent a party, led by Sergeant Fury, up the hill in pursuit. As he reached the crest of the hill, Fury was hit in the chest by a Cree bullet, but his men continued, killing several Cree fighters.

One of Steele's Scouts wounded a native fighter, a Woods Cree who was carrying a note from W. J. McLean. The note said the Woods Cree were tired of fighting and running. They wanted to surrender along with the captives, leaving Big Bear and his Plains Cree followers to head for the US border several hundred kilometres away. It seemed that Big Bear's support was crumbling from within. But the Cree leader wasn't ready to give up the fight.

Eventually the Cree and their prisoners retreated across the narrow, shallow stretch of water behind their camp and ran into the heavy bush. From there, they continued firing as the Scouts advanced. Low on ammunition, Sam called for a ceasefire and again summoned Canon MacKay to call for Big Bear to surrender. For a tense moment, silence reigned. Then the angry voices of the Cree fighters rang out, and they started firing again.

Despite the Cree's defiance, Sam knew his quarry was pinned in the woods. But his men were outnumbered, so he decided to wait until Middleton arrived to support a final charge. He sent a sergeant back along the trail to guide the advancing army, but the sergeant returned to report there was no advancing army — no sign at all. With limited ammunition and food, Sam had no choice but to withdraw. Bitterly he ordered his men to fall back.

As the Scouts reluctantly retreated, Sam posted several men as a rear guard overlooking Loon Lake. Suddenly the Scouts spotted movement in the forest across the narrows, just making out two men moving through the bush. Mistaking the men for Cree, they fired but missed. The men ducked, then disappeared into the woods. Those men, the Scouts later learned, were McLean and another captive who were attempting to contact the Scouts and negotiate a ceasefire. Again the Scouts had missed a chance to rescue the hostages.

While they waited for Strange and Middleton, Sam and his men were forced to let the Cree get away. They waited until June 5. Though Middleton gave half-hearted chase, Big Bear and his Plains Cree followers slipped away. To Sam's amazement and disgust, Middleton then ordered the entire force to retreat to Fort Pitt. There, Steele's Scouts languished for a month before they were ordered back to Calgary.

To Sam and his men, it seemed an inglorious end to their brave campaign. In their minds, the Cree got away with murder, and the hostages were still captive. What had Steele's Scouts and General Strange's militia accomplished? Frustrated, the men did as they were commanded and traced their route south.

A Hero's Welcome

In fact, Steele's Scouts were victorious, though they didn't know it until they got to Calgary. After the battle at Loon Lake, the Cree had split into various groups, melting away into the vast woodland. Big Bear himself went south, but his followers abandoned him. Eventually he was accompanied by only a handful of family members and supporters. Wandering Spirit and the Woods Cree released the hostages, who were found in the bush near Fort Pitt, weary but unharmed.

But the citizens of Calgary knew that Sam and his Scouts had defeated the Cree, and Steele's Scouts were hailed as conquering heroes as they rode into the city. The mayor held a banquet in their honour, and the city presented Sam with a diamond ring as a gift of gratitude. Sam would later write that the Scouts were "the best body of men I have ever had anything to do with."

Wandering Spirit gave himself up at Fort Pitt and was hanged for his part in the murders of the settlers and priests at Frog Lake and the killing of NWMP Constable Cowan at Fort Pitt. Big Bear eluded police and soldiers for some time but was arrested when he arrived in Fort Carlton looking for food. He was jailed for three years.

Steele's Scouts were officially disbanded upon their return to Calgary. Sam went back to his life in the

NWMP, now promoted to the rank of superintendent. In his absence, the railway construction camps had reverted to their wild ways, so Sam set up his quarters at Revelstoke, at the end of track. He spent the rest of the summer of 1885 getting things back in order along the rail line and in the construction camps.

At last, on November 7, 1885, a small group of dignitaries, including Sam, gathered in the mountains west of Revelstoke to see the CPR's president, Donald Smith, pound home the CPR's last spike. Then the officials boarded a waiting train, bound for Vancouver. A guest of the CPR as a reward for his part in the railway's construction, Sam thoroughly enjoyed the journey, which was his first trip to the coast. He loved the magnificent landscapes, the long tunnels, and high trestles. Although his holiday was brief — he was back in Calgary within a week — it was an exciting way to cap the three years he'd spent policing CPR construction across the West.

Chapter 4
Sam the Negotiator

t was 1887, and Sam Steele, now 36, had survived disease and gun battles and faced angry mobs of all sorts. Through fearless action, he earned the admiration of everyone who crossed his path.

In his next adventure, Sam exhibited decisiveness of a different kind — as a savvy negotiator.

Chief Isadore's Troubles

The southwestern flank of the Rockies — a region called Kootenay after the area's indigenous people — was known for its gold. Though the Kootenay gold claims weren't as rich as other areas of British Columbia, there was enough gold to lure prospectors and settlers to the Columbia Valley and its surrounding mountains. The Kootenay First Nation was at first welcoming, but as more settlers moved into the region, they became wary, fearing their way of life was under threat.

Tensions in the area had been escalating since the unsolved murder of two miners in 1884. In 1887, though they had no hard evidence, the local provincial police arrested a Kootenay man named Kapla and charged him with the crime. Kapla was jailed at Wild Horse Creek, a tiny prospector's settlement. Isadore, chief of the local Kootenay band, was furious and led 20 warriors to free Kapla. With Kapla liberated, Isadore threatened the constable and justice of the peace with death if they remained at Wild Horse. The two men quickly vacated, leaving the area's ranchers, settlers, and miners feeling defenceless and worried about what might happen next.

The Kootenay also claimed that their reserve lands were too small. Local ranchers owned all the good grazing land, including the Kootenay's traditional hunting and pasturing land, leaving precious little grazing for the Kootenay's cattle and horses. In addition, a local landowner who'd allowed the Kootenay to graze their livestock on his land had died. The new owner, Colonel

James Baker, was not receptive to the agreement, ordering Isadore to get his cattle off the property. Isadore
declined.

Isadore's young warriors were angry, defiant, and
restless. Tempers and tensions mounted on both sides.
Fearing an uprising, NWMP Commissioner Herchmer
ordered Sam to take a division of men from Fort Macleod
across the mountains to keep the peace. Sam and his
men departed in June 1887, bound for Kootenay country — the hard way.

Like many of Sam's travels, his trip to the Kootenay
region was challenging. Though their destination was
less than 350 kilometres west of Fort Macleod, there was
no trail over the Rockies. Instead, Sam's men, horses,
and supplies headed for Calgary, where they boarded a
train bound west to Golden on the Columbia River. Sam
then prepared his men to ride south along the Columbia
to the Kootenay district, while sending their supplies on
board the *Duchess*, a paddlewheeler. Before the troops
left Golden though, tragedy struck. Troubled by debilitating medical problems, one of Sam's men committed
suicide. To make matters worse, the *Duchess* sank just a
few kilometres south of Golden, taking with it the
troops' supplies and personal belongings.

Undaunted, Sam hired another steamer and found
enough replacement supplies to get the expedition

under way. On July 18, he and his men started their trek south, arriving at Galbraith's Ferry, a tiny settlement on the banks of the Kootenay River, on July 30. Under Sam's direction, the men set to work sawing and hauling logs, constructing a new NWMP post. His experience overseeing the building of several posts paid off. The new fort, which Sam called Kootenay Post, was the best built of all the NWMP posts — and it was completed in less than three weeks.

Sam the Negotiator

Sam was quick to invite Chief Isadore to visit the new fort while construction was still under way, but Isadore took his time and didn't arrive at Kootenay Post until mid-August. All Sam's skills as a forthright negotiator came into play. Sam told Isadore he would not press charges for helping Kapla break out of jail if the fugitive was handed over to the police immediately. Kapla promptly found himself back in the Wild Horse jail.

On August 25, Sam went to Wild Horse, where he held a preliminary hearing into the murder charge against Kapla. He then had the prisoner transferred to Kootenay Post and set a trial date, September 5. Sam presided over Kapla's case, but after only a short hearing, he dismissed it for lack of evidence. He handed out food to Kapla and his supporters for their journey back to the reserve and sent them on their way.

Isadore himself was present at the trial and seemed impressed by Sam's fairness. However, the Kootenay leader remained uneasy about the mounted police presence in his territory. Isadore was afraid the red coats had a secret motive — war against the Kootenay people. Sam said, "I informed him that such was not the case. I came here to maintain law and order, both white and Indians were all the same to us, and would be fairly treated, but that any breach of the law would be severely dealt with, no matter who the offender might be."

Negotiations continued, testing both Sam's patience and skill to the limit. The government increased the Kootenay's reserve lands, but the expansion did not include Colonel Baker's land. Isadore was insulted but Sam stood firm. Isadore reluctantly agreed to the new reserve boundaries, then changed his mind. Sam was exasperated but held his temper, telling Isadore that the chief was behaving shamefully.

Next the government agreed to pay Isadore for fences and other improvements he'd made to Baker's land under the previous owner. Isadore told Sam the fences were worth $1000, a ridiculous sum. Again Sam had to carefully negotiate, telling Isadore the amount was far too high, without angering the leader and

A composite picture of the NWMP and native groups.
Sam Steele is pictured in the middle row on the left.

triggering a revolt. Sam paid Isadore $490 and the matter seemed to be settled at last — but it wasn't.

The smouldering dispute between Isadore and Baker erupted again in the spring of 1888. Colonel Baker, who had been in Victoria for the winter, returned to find Isadore's cattle on his property, as well as new fences and shacks. Baker was furious. He invited Isadore to the ranch, intending to ride the ranch's perimeter with the native leader and clearly establish the boundaries. Isadore went to the meeting, but during the ride, the two men quarrelled and Sam was once again called to resolve the dispute. At the end of his patience, Sam threatened that Isadore would be replaced as chief of the Kootenay. Isadore at last promised not to trespass on Baker's land anymore.

Before returning to Fort Macleod, Sam organized a sports day for all the region's residents. The day was a great success and went a long way to paving smooth relations between the residents. At day's end, Isadore gave a speech praising Sam and the mounted police, saying their actions and fair treatment had done much to dissolve the distrust between settlers and the Kootenay people. For his part, Sam later called Isadore "the most powerful chief I met in my forty years of service."

With the disputes settled, the police left the

Kootenay district on August 7, 1888. On the return to Fort Macleod, Sam and his men pioneered a route across the Rockies. Instead of returning to Golden and taking the train back to Calgary, the troops rode up the Elk River valley and through the Crowsnest Pass. While the same journey the previous summer had taken a month to complete, they covered the distance to Fort Macleod in just nine days, proving the usefulness of the Crowsnest route should they have to return to the Kootenay area in a hurry. But they never did.

Romance and Marriage

After his return from the Kootenay district, Sam was in charge of Fort Macleod and the surrounding territory in southern Alberta. Although there was still plenty of policing work to take care of, the next 10 years were relatively quiet for Sam. He even found time for romance.

In 1889, Marie Elizabeth Harwood waltzed into Sam Steele's life. That summer, she was in Fort Macleod visiting her aunt, the wife of a superintendent under Sam's command. Marie was 29, tall and slender, with dark hair and a pleasant appearance. Fort Macleod was a departure from her normally quiet life amid well-heeled Quebec society, but she loved the West. She was especially charmed by the fort's famous commanding officer, the towering Sam Steele. The two began a relaxed courtship, a true summer romance. Sam enjoyed telling stories and found a willing audience in Marie, who was thrilled by his tales. They went to the many local dances, and Sam also took Marie to less formal events — rodeos, polo and cricket matches, parties, and card games. Much to Sam's delight, Marie loved horses and was an excellent rider, and they often took evening rides together.

There was a fly in the ointment, though. Sam was from a poor rural Ontario background and was a staunch Anglican, while Marie was a wealthy French-speaking Roman Catholic. Her father was a member of Parliament and her mother's family had been in Quebec since French colonial times. Some of Sam's friends advised him against getting further involved, but his mind was made up. Sam proposed to Marie and she eagerly accepted.

Sam and Marie were married in Quebec on January 15, 1890. After his many years of service, Sam had a great deal of vacation owing, so the couple took a long honeymoon trip. First they went to New York. Typically, Sam had made arrangements to visit the New York Police, who turned Sam's visit into an occasion complete with 60 fire engines on parade. The couple continued their trip throughout the eastern states, then went to Ottawa, where Sam at last met Prime Minister Sir John A. Macdonald. Finally the newlyweds returned to Fort Macleod in May.

Sam and Marie had an active social life that included dances, dinners, and musical evenings, and Sam often took his new wife along on his police patrols. The couple soon had two girls; a boy followed a few years later. This idyllic life continued until 1898, when Sam received orders that sent him on another frontier adventure.

Chapter 5
The Yukon and Beyond

In 1896, gold was discovered in the Klondike region of the Yukon Territory. Fortune seekers began pouring in from all over the world, and the North-West Mounted Police already in the North were vastly outnumbered by the hordes of people. The police were also outgunned by the criminal element eagerly following the prospectors. The Yukon was virtually lawless. It was a situation tailor-made for Sam Steele.

Land of the Midnight Sun
In January 1898, Sam received urgent orders to proceed

to the Yukon. His orders commanded him to leave immediately for Vancouver, where he would receive further instructions. Not knowing when he would return, Sam left his family in Fort Macleod and got to Vancouver on January 31. There, he was greeted by NWMP Superintendent Bowen Perry, who had Sam's orders direct from Clifford Sifton, minister of the interior.

The two men were to establish NWMP outposts at the summits of the White and Chilkoot Passes, the notoriously difficult gateways to the Yukon. The exact location of the Alaska–Yukon border was in dispute — Canada maintained that the passes marked the border, while the US claimed the border was farther east, therefore both passes were well inside its own territory. Sam and Perry were to claim the territory for Canada.

Perry left immediately for Alaska, but there were so many gold seekers passing through Vancouver that Sam had to wait a week. While Sam was waiting, Superintendent Perry was busy in the Yukon, establishing police outposts at the tops of both passes. At first the NWMP posts consisted only of tents, enough food for the winter, and machine guns, but the men stationed at each post started to build cabins despite extreme cold weather and heavy snow. Their objectives were to get the cabins built and to raise the Canadian flag (the Union Jack at that time), clearly claiming the territory as Canadian soil — the Dominion government was also eager for the police officers to start collecting customs duties.

There was enormous potential for customs revenue. The Yukon's commissioner decreed that no gold seeker would be allowed into the territory unless he brought a year's worth of supplies — food, clothing, camping gear, and so on. As a result, would-be prospectors spent weeks ferrying supplies over one of the high mountain passes and down to Lake Bennett, where they camped to wait out the winter. It could take up to 40 trips to get all the required supplies and equipment into the Yukon. Now they would be greeted at the passes by Canadian police officers intent on taxing every item.

Sam finally reached Skagway, Alaska, on February 13. As the starting point for the gold seekers' route, Skagway was where they bought supplies before heading up either of the passes. It was a ramshackle town of saloons, brothels, card parlours, and honky-tonks with a transient population of around 5000. Sam called it "about the roughest place in the world," with the town's criminal element being dominated by Soapy Smith and his thugs.

On February 16, Perry returned to Skagway to meet Sam and report on his progress. Construction of both posts was under way, but the flags weren't yet flying. Perry was on his way back to the summit of the White

Pass to review progress and see the flag flying for himself, while Sam and his assistant, Constable Skirving, headed for the Chilkoot Pass to do the same thing.

Sam and Skirving took a boat from Skagway to the town of Dyea at the trailhead. On February 17, they started their trek on the Chilkoot Trail in a howling blizzard, struggling up the extremely steep slope. By noon, they reached the temporary stables of a company hauling supplies to the top of the pass. They could go no farther and stopped for a hot meal and shelter from the storm.

The next morning, Sam and Skirving continued, though the storm was still raging. They reached Sheep Camp, a relatively level area where gold seekers staged their supplies for the final push to the Chilkoot summit. The two men attempted to reach the summit, but the storm pushed them back. They decided to take shelter at a construction camp they'd passed on their way up the trail, but by the time they turned back, the camp was almost impossible to find — the tents were buried in snow.

The following morning, they were preparing for another attempt when a constable from the summit outpost arrived to report that the cabin had been hastily completed and the police outpost was ready to begin operation. Sam sent the man back to the pass with orders to get the flag flying and begin operations as a customs post.

For the moment, that was all the information Sam needed. Obeying orders from Minister Sifton, Sam immediately returned to Skagway and sent a telegram to Ottawa, informing the minister that the Chilkoot post was in operation and the territory firmly claimed for Canada.

Technically Sam's mission was accomplished, but he knew his job wasn't over. He spent the next few weeks in Skagway buying supplies that the NWMP posts would need in the coming year. Meanwhile, the posts atop both passes were doing a booming business, collecting 25 percent duty on all items not purchased in Canada — which was virtually everything every gold seeker sought to transport into Canadian territory.

Near the end of March, Sam received word that the officer in command of the White Pass post was gravely ill with bronchitis. Sam had bronchitis himself, but was determined to relieve the officer. He arrived to find the post surrounded by piles of the gold seekers' supplies awaiting customs inspection. Sam stayed for several days to help clear the backlog, then headed down the east side of the pass to Lake Bennett, where he intended to set up NWMP headquarters for the region.

"The Wonderful Exodus of Boats Began."
As he approached Lake Bennett, Sam passed the temporary camps of thousands of gold seekers in the process of getting their supplies from Skagway over the passes and into the Yukon. While they waited for the spring thaw, the would-be prospectors were also building the rafts and boats they would use to continue to the Klondike.

Sam took up residence in a log shack on the lakeshore. Here he spent the next two months, commanding a small contingent of police. Most of his duties involved settling disputes and keeping the peace in the tent city that had gradually materialized on Lake Bennett's shore.

Although the tent city was well inside Canadian territory, Soapy Smith's criminal gang from Skagway eventually arrived on the scene. One evening, two shots rang out and Sam sent a sergeant to investigate. The police officer found a man who claimed his gun had discharged accidentally, but when the sergeant searched the man's supplies, he discovered a deck of marked cards. The sergeant arrested the card shark and dragged him to the police cabin. When he was taken into Sam's office, the prisoner yelled, "I'll have you know you can't lock up a United States citizen and get away with it!" to which Sam replied, "Well, since you're an American citizen I'll be lenient. I'll confiscate all your goods and give you half an hour to leave town." The man was immediately escorted to the border, 35 kilometres away.

Sam's reputation alone was a formidable deterrent to crime in the tent city. One day, a bank manager on his way to open a branch of the Imperial Bank of Canada in Dawson City came into police headquarters. The man was carrying $2 million in cash, which he asked Sam to guard until his northward journey could continue after the spring breakup. Lacking a safe, strongbox, or other suitable hiding place, Sam stashed the cash under his bed of rough planks and straw. Although it was probably common knowledge there was a large amount of money in the police cabin, nobody dared challenge the towering Sam Steele. The money remained untouched for several months, and when Lake Bennett was free of ice, the bank manager claimed his cash and went on his way.

As Sam patrolled the tent city, observing the makeshift watercrafts the gold seekers were building, he became concerned about the seaworthiness of many vessels. He issued an edict that every boat built in the Lake Bennett community must be registered, along with the names and home addresses of everyone who intended to ride in the boat. If a boat went down, Sam wanted to know exactly who had gone down with it.

The fierce weather continued well into the spring

months. On April 27, an avalanche buried 63 gold seekers who were toiling up the west side of Chilkoot Pass. Although the tragedy occurred on the American side, Sam ordered the men from the NWMP border outpost at the summit to help recover the dead and to make sure Soapy Smith's gang did not loot or steal the victims' belongings. Sam compiled a list of the dead and personally wrote to their families, whether they were Canadian, American, British, or citizens of other countries.

Finally on May 29 the lake ice broke and the gold rush was on. Sam wrote, "The wonderful exodus of boats began. I went up to the hill behind the office to see the start, and at one time counted 800 boats under sail in the eleven and a half miles of Lake Bennett." Sam himself departed that day on board a small steamer. He travelled the length of Lake Bennett and down the Yukon River, but he didn't get far. After just 80 kilometres, the engine malfunctioned and the boat was stranded for a day.

When his journey resumed, Sam arrived at Miles Canyon, where the Yukon River rushes over 8-kilometre-long Whitehorse Rapids. The previous year, the roaring waters had claimed 200 lives; even the day before, when Sam was stranded upriver, 5 people drowned and 150 boats were destroyed in the rapids. At the canyon's mouth, Sam encountered a logjam of boats waiting their

Sam Steele running the rapids of Miles Canyon
on board the steamer *Willie Irving*

turn to run the rapids — he needed to take action to avoid more deaths. Never afraid to make up laws when the situation called for it, Sam summoned all the gold seekers to a meeting. A crowd gathered to hear what the big red-coated man had to say.

Sam first declared that no women or children would be allowed to travel by boat through the canyon — they had to walk to the other end of the rapids. Further, no boat would be allowed to run the rapids until the police were satisfied that both the boat and its owner were capable of reaching the other end. Sam then selected a number of river pilots who could safely steer the boats if the owners were deemed incompetent to run the white water. He set a $100 fine for anyone who breached this impromptu law. The gold seekers grumbled but complied. Through the course of the summer, approximately 7000 boats ran the rapids without the loss of another life.

San Francisco of the North

Sam finally closed his Lake Bennett office and headed to Dawson City, arriving there in September 1898 to find it "a city of chaos" — and not entirely because of crime. Dawson had been hastily settled two years before on swampy land. Drainage was poor and the town flooded frequently. As a result of inadequate sanitation, a typhoid epidemic swept through the population, claiming 84 lives.

That year, Dawson City had a population of about 14,000 (today there are about 2000 residents). Along with the prospectors had come the usual assortment of riffraff, prostitutes, gamblers, and crooks. With only 13 police stationed in Dawson, Sam and his men were constantly busy in this wild town, known as San Francisco of the North. Upon his arrival, Sam ordered an expansion of the local jail, then put prisoners to work on various community service tasks.

Realizing that his men needed assistance, Sam enlisted the help of the Canadian army's Yukon Field Force and found himself commanding an extra 70 soldiers. He deployed the soldiers in various ways, mostly as guards at banks and government buildings. From his police force, he selected several men as undercover agents who kept an eye on the bars and dance halls. As a result, many thieves and crooks found life in Dawson too hot and disappeared.

Those who stuck around were frequently arrested for the smallest crimes and given a "blue ticket" — an order to leave town. A convicted criminal who ignored the blue ticket got up to six months in prison. One of Sam's favourite projects for the jail's inmates was the infamous woodpile, where the jailbirds were put to work chopping and splitting wood. "That woodpile was the talk of the town, and kept 50 or more toughs of Dawson busy every day," he later wrote.

Although Dawson's two tiny hospitals were full of typhoid victims, the Yukon government was short of money to improve sanitation and health care. To deal with the situation, Sam established a board of health, of which he was chairman. Conveniently, he was also the chief of police and a magistrate. As punishment for various crimes, Sam exacted enormous fines, with the proceeds going straight to caring for typhoid patients. The following spring, he made prisoners dig drainage ditches and collect garbage to avoid another typhoid outbreak, with much success — the number of cases dropped dramatically.

Sam was also chairman of the board responsible for issuing business licences for everything from hotels to casinos. He established especially steep fees for bars and saloons. In six months, he collected about $90,000, which he forwarded to the territorial authorities. This revenue kept the Yukon government from declaring bankruptcy, but the high cost of obtaining a liquor licence had another benefit — seedy operators couldn't afford to open a bar. "Dives and low drinking dens are a thing of the past, never to return," Sam wrote in his year-end report for 1898, adding, "Any man, woman or child may walk at any time of the night to any portion of this large camp with as much personal safety from insult as on Sparks Street in Ottawa."

As when he policed the CPR construction camps in the 1880s, Sam governed Dawson City with intelligence, using equal measures of muscle and restraint. He wasn't terribly worried about the newly wealthy prospectors who freely spent their money in the bars and casinos.

Hardened criminals were Sam's main concern — his goal was to keep violence and organized crime out of the Yukon. He even looked the other way when it came to prostitution. As long as prostitutes remained within the red light districts, Sam left them alone.

For his fair dealings, honesty, and iron fist when it came to crime, Sam earned the respect of Dawson's residents and the admiration of the men under his command. His men worked extremely hard, but he worked even harder. He wrote, "My working hours were at least 19. I retired to rest about two a.m. or later, rose at six, was out of doors at seven, walked five miles up the Klondyke on the ice and back over the mountain, visited every institution under me each day, sat on boards and committees until midnight, attended to the routine of the Yukon command without an adjutant, saw every prisoner daily, and was in the town station after midnight to see how things were going." And he was approaching 50.

Perhaps Sam's time in the Yukon lacked the stirring battles and first-hand interaction with outlaws that had marked his earlier years, but this was the pinnacle of Sam's career. He faced extreme weather, overcame organized crime, and negotiated and settled disputes. He dispensed justice and established community services that greatly improved the life of Dawson's residents.

Sam was a topnotch police officer in every way. In fact, he was a little too good.

End of the Ride

Ironically, the most difficult problem Sam faced in the Yukon was government corruption. A large number of falsified records and claims went missing or were incorrectly registered, to the benefit of what Sam called "wolves in sheep's clothing who cheated the decent miner of his hard-earned claims." But because many territory administrators had been appointed by the Dominion government, Sam was powerless to stop the widespread graft and thievery.

One notorious figure was J. D. McGregor, the Yukon's inspector of mines, who'd been appointed by Clifford Sifton, the same minister who had ordered Sam to the Yukon. McGregor's position allowed him to extract kickbacks and other favours, but he was virtually above the law. When Sifton tried to give his friend McGregor responsibility for issuing liquor licences as well, Sam led a group of concerned Dawson citizens in opposition. This action pitted Sam against Minister Sifton, who had ultimate authority over the NWMP.

Sam's political face-off with Sifton gave McGregor and many other shady government officials the chance they were waiting for. They complained to Sifton that Sam was in charge of the Yukon, overstepping his authority and running affairs far beyond the reach of the police. A deputation of Yukon officials went to Ottawa to personally state their claims against Sam. Sifton took action, relieving Sam of his duties in the Yukon in September 1899. In a terse telegram dated September 8, Sam received orders to immediately leave Dawson and report to NWMP headquarters in Regina.

As news of Sam's impending departure spread, the people of Dawson reacted with shock and anger. The local newspapers joined the chorus of indignation, all rising in Sam's defence against his political adversaries. One editor even went so far as to send a telegram to Prime Minister Sir Wilfred Laurier, saying, "For the good of government beseech you to suspend order removing Colonel Steele from command here. Will be terrible blunder." But Laurier denied knowledge of Sam's removal, saying Sifton had control over mounted police matters.

Dawson's leading citizens then hastily circulated a petition. On September 16, a crowd of 500 gathered at the Criterion Theatre to protest Sam's recall from Dawson. Among those attending were miners and prospectors who had walked from their far-flung gold claims to speak on Sam's behalf. The delegation drafted a resolution that read "… dissatisfaction of the entire population of this Territory at this, the removal of our most popular and trusted official. It would be a direct injury to the Territory should he be taken away." The resolution was circulated far and wide, signed by thousands of people before it was sent to Ottawa.

For his part, though, Sam was exhausted. He called his sojourn in the Yukon "the most difficult that has ever fallen to the lot of a member of the NWMP." He had been away from his wife and family since January 1898, more than 18 months. He told the citizens of Dawson, "On no account would any influence induce me to remain unless I were ordered, and even then it would be against my will."

And so, despite all the telegrams, petitions, letters, and protests, Sam made plans to leave Dawson on September 26. On that day, hundreds of people went to the docks to see him board the steamer that would take him up the Yukon River to Lake Bennett. Miners and mounted police, gamblers and saloon keepers, they all went to wish him well. A man named Big Alex McDonald was chosen to give a speech. He held a bag of gold nuggets, a gift collected from the many citizens on both sides of the law who had grown to respect Sam. Normally not lost for words, McDonald was so overcome on this occasion that he didn't know what to say except "Here, Sam, here you are. Poke for you. Goodbye," as he thrust the bag of gold into Sam's hand.

As Sam's steamer cast off, the crowd called out their farewells, and boat bells and whistles joined the chorus. Sam Steele left the Yukon on a wave of cheers and applause that lasted until the boat was well out of sight.

Chapter 6
Sam at War

fter his tour of duty in the Yukon came to a sudden end in September 1899, Sam joined his family, who had moved to Montreal. He was at loose ends — but not for long. His adventures weren't over yet.

Although Sam remained an officer in the NWMP, he heeded the call to action in support of British interests in South Africa. Sam's skills as a scout and tracker, and his experience fighting a crafty adversary in thick bush, made him the obvious choice for a series of challenges far beyond Canada's borders.

Fighting Sam

By January 1900, the Boer War was raging in South Africa, and Canada sent troops to the conflict. When the army offered Sam the command of a new fighting cavalry unit, he jumped at the chance. He named the unit Lord Strathcona's Horse in honour of the cavalry's patron, Donald Smith, Lord Strathcona.

Volunteers for the new cavalry unit came from all over western Canada. Even a group of American cowboys offered to bring their own horses and supplies for a chance to ride into battle under the famous Sam Steele (he had to turn them down). The 500 men and 600 horses of Lord Strathcona's Horse departed for South Africa in March 1900. When General Kitchener, the commanding officer in South Africa, first saw Sam and his cavalry, he commented on how large the frontier men were. Sam replied, "My apologies, Sir. I combed all of Canada, and these are the smallest I could find."

Sam Steele and Lord Strathcona's Horse had numerous exploits in South Africa and earned widespread respect. London newspapers referred to him as "Fighting Sam" and "the world's greatest scout." For his actions and work in South Africa, Sam was decorated by King Edward VII. He returned to Canada a hero — but before long, he was back in South Africa to oversee the establishment and training of a new police force, the

South African Constabulary.

When Sam returned to Canada in 1906, the Steeles settled in Winnipeg. During the next several years, Sam wrote an autobiography. The book, *Forty Years in Canada — Reminiscences of the Great Northwest,* was published in 1915, but by that time he was already off on another adventure.

When World War I erupted in Europe, 63-year-old Sam immediately volunteered for active military duty. Although he was qualified, experienced, physically fit, and probably the most famous soldier in Canada, he was almost passed over because of his age. But public outcry and Sam's own agitation to be given a military post prevailed, and at virtually the last minute, he was given the military rank of major-general and put in command of a new corps, the Second Canadian Overseas Division. With 25,000 men under him, this was the largest command in Sam's life.

Sam shipped out to England, where he trained Canadian troops for active combat in France. In the midst of the raging war, he was knighted on January 1, 1918. Six months later, he officially retired. When the war ended on November 11, 1918, Sam and his family planned to stay in England for a few months, then return to either Winnipeg or Calgary. But influenza was sweeping through Europe and Sam caught the dreaded disease.

Sam at War

Sir Samuel Benfield Steele died in London of influenza on January 30, 1919, a few weeks after his 68th birthday. Sam had been present at virtually every major event in western Canada from 1874 to 1900. He'd faced down Cree, Blood, Blackfoot, and Kootenay chiefs and warriors. He'd traded gunfire with fugitives, thieves, whisky traders, and murderers. And he'd survived everything from quicksand to Rocky Mountain fever, but influenza was the one enemy he couldn't defeat. His funeral procession in London included contingents from the North-West Mounted Police, Lord Strathcona's Horse, and the Second Canadian Overseas Division of the Canadian armed forces.

Sam wanted to be buried in Winnipeg, but because there were so many troops going home from Europe, it was months before his body could be transported to Canada. Even in death, Sam managed to participate in a major western Canadian event — the Winnipeg General Strike. His coffin was held at the mounted police headquarters while street fighting and rioting exploded outside. The next morning, there was a second funeral for Sam, the largest ever in western Canada at that time. Despite the tension between striking workers and the police, there was no trouble during the funeral, and Sam was laid to rest in Winnipeg's St. John's Cemetery.

Epilogue
Sam Steele's Legacy

Besides the stories and legends of his amazing life, reminders of Sam Steele are scattered across western Canada.

• After Sam and the NWMP departed from Kootenay Post in 1888, a town grew up around the fort. The citizens officially changed the town's name to Fort Steele, although Sam protested, writing at the time, "I have very great objections to anything of this kind." The town was once home to 1500 people, but the population gradually decreased and Fort Steele became a ghost town. Then in 1961 the BC government began a restoration program to create a provincial historical site. Today, Fort Steele Heritage Town is one of BC's most popular heritage attractions. Among the more than 60 historical buildings is the original NWMP officers quarters from Kootenay Post, where Sam lived and worked for more than a year. This building houses artifacts that include Sam's uniform and pistol.

• At 5073 metres, Mount Steele is Canada's sixth-highest mountain. It is in the Yukon's lofty St. Elias Range, in Kluane National Park.

• Lord Strathcona's Horse served in South Africa's Boer War, both world wars, and Korea. Today, Lord Strathcona's Horse has many responsibilities, including serving in United Nations peacekeeping missions and NATO operations.

• The memory of Steele's Scouts is alive and well, too. In 1977, a group of history-minded horsemen throughout southern Alberta decided to re-create Steele's Scouts. The modern-day Steele's Scouts dress in replicas of the original uniform — the buckskin jackets and Stetson-style hats — and carry working replicas of 1880s rifles or sidearms. They perform riding drills and manoeuvres at the Calgary Stampede, Spruce Meadows, Calgary's Heritage Park, and numerous small-town events, rodeos, and celebrations. The 80 members also carry out commemorative long-distance trail rides that trace the paths of Sam Steele's adventures.

• Sam Steele was a trained fighting man and handy with both a pistol and a rifle, but he did not believe that violence was the way to resolve disputes, preferring instead to negotiate. His leadership, in the NWMP and the Canadian military, earned him the devotion of his men and the admiration of the citizens he served. Sam was the embodiment of integrity, a quality embraced by the entire NWMP and an ongoing legacy. The reputation for honesty and fairness that's carried on by the Royal Canadian Mounted Police started with Sam Steele and endures to this day — perhaps that's the best tribute of all.

Bibliography

Beahen, William and Stan Horrall. *Red Coats on the Prairies — The North-West Mounted Police 1886–1900*. Regina, SK: Friends of the Mounted Police Museum and PrintWest Publishing Services, 1998.

Berton, Pierre. *The Great Railway*. Toronto: McClelland and Stewart, 1972.

Brown, Wayne E. *Steele's Scouts: Samuel Benfield Steele and the North-West Rebellion*. Surrey, BC: Heritage House, 2001.

Miller, Naomi. *Fort Steele: Gold Rush to Boom Town*. Surrey, BC: Heritage House, 2002.

Neufeld, David and Frank Norris. *Chilkoot Trail: Heritage Route to the Klondike*. Whitehorse: Lost Moose, The Yukon Publishers, 1996.

Ross, Martin. "The Boom & Bust of Fort Steele, A Self-Guided Visit to the Real Western Frontier." Fort Steele Heritage Town Archives and British Columbia Ministry of Community, Aboriginal and Women's Services.

Stewart, Robert. *Sam Steele: Lion of the Frontier.* 2nd ed. Regina, SK: Friends of the Mounted Police Museum and Centax Books Publishing Solutions/PrintWest Group, 1999.

Woodward, Meredith Bain and Robert Woodward. *British Columbia Interior, An Altitude SuperGuide.* Canmore, AB: Altitude Publishing, 2003.

Acknowledgments

The author acknowledges the following sources for the quotes contained in this book: the excellent work of Robert Stewart and his book *Sam Steele: Lion of the Frontier;* Wayne Brown, author of *Steele's Scouts: Samuel Benfield Steele and the North-West Rebellion;* and Naomi Miller's book, *Fort Steele: Gold Rush to Boom Town.* These fine books in turn quote from Sam Steele's autobiography, *Forty Years in Canada.* A visit to Fort Steele Heritage Town was also invaluable in helping me gain a vivid picture of Sam Steele's life. Thanks as ever to my laughing partner Ken Wong, who willingly shared our home with another man — Sam Steele — during the researching and writing of this book.

About the Author

Holly Quan lives in the foothills of southwestern Alberta among the poplars and coyotes. She's the author of two titles in the Amazing Stories series and two guide books, in addition to writing magazine articles on travel, food, horses, marketing, and whatever else piques her interest. When she's not working on her novel manuscript — a work now many years in the making — she loves to ski, ride, hike, swim, drink wine with her friends, and howl at the moon.

OTHER AMAZING STORIES

ISBN	Title	Author
1-55153-977-2	Air Force War Heroes	Cynthia Faryon
1-55153-983-7	Alberta Titans	Susan Warrender
1-55153-982-9	Dinosaur Hunters	Lisa Murphy-Lamb
1-55153-970-5	Early Voyageurs	Marie Savage
1-55153-968-3	Edwin Alonzo Boyd	Nate Hendley
1-55153-996-9	Emily Carr	Cat Klerks
1-55153-992-6	Ghost Town Stories from the Red Coat Trail	Johnnie Bachusky
1-55153-993-4	Ghost Town Stories from the Canadian Rockies	Johnnie Bachusky
1-55153-969-1	Klondike Joe Boyle	Stan Sauerwein
1-55153-979-9	Ma Murray	Stan Sauerwein
1-55153-999-3	Mary Schäffer	Jill Foran
1-55153-962-4	Niagara Daredevils	Cheryl MacDonald
1-55153-981-0	Rattenbury	Stan Sauerwein
1-55153-991-8	Rebel Women	Linda Kupecek
1-55153-995-0	Rescue Dogs	Dale Portman
1-55153-998-5	Romance in the Rockies	Kim Mayberry
1-55153-985-3	Tales from the Backcountry	Dale Portman
1-55153-986-1	Tales from the West Coast	Adrienne Mason
1-55153-994-2	The Heart of a Horse	Gayle Bunney
1-55153-989-6	Vancouver's Old-Time Scoundrels	Jill Foran
1-55153-987-X	Wilderness Tales	Peter Christensen
1-55153-990-X	West Coast Adventures	Adrienne Mason
1-55153-980-2	Women Explorers	Helen Rolfe

These titles are available wherever you buy books. If you have trouble finding the book you want, call the Altitude order desk at 1-800-957-6888, e-mail your request to: orderdesk@altitudepublishing.com or visit our Web site at www.amazingstories.ca

All titles retail for $9.95 Cdn or $7.95 US. (Prices subject to change.)

New AMAZING STORIES titles are published every month. If you would like more information, e-mail your name and mailing address to: amazingstories@altitudepublishing.com.